The Word Seen and Touched

*Lectio Divina and
Human Experience*

The Word Seen and Touched

Lectio Divina and
Human Experience

BRENDAN CLIFFORD OP

DOMINICAN PUBLICATIONS

Published (2013) by
Dominican Publications
42 Parnell Square
Dublin 1

ISBN 978-1-905604-27-2
British Library Cataloguing in Publications Data
A cataloguing record for this book is available from the British Library.

Origination by Dominican Publications

Cover and book design by David Cooke

Printed in Ireland by
SprintPrint Ltd
Rathcoole
Co. Dublin

Contents

Lectio divina brings you into direct conversation
    with the Lord
and it opens for you wisdom's treasure.
The intimate friendship with the One who loves us
enables us to see with the eyes of God,
to speak with his Word in our hearts,
to treasure the beauty of that experience and
to share it with those who are hungry for eternity.

Pope Francis
5 September 2013

Acknowledgments

Since 1985 I have been slowly learning about lectio divina and have been teaching it to small groups. It has been my principal task since I came to the Dominican Biblical Institute in Limerick in 2000. In 2001 Fr Diarmuid Clifford, editor of the *St Martin's Magazine*, invited me to write a monthly lectio divina meditation. In the following year Fr Joseph Kavanagh asked me to write an Introduction to Lectio Divina for the Priory Institute in Tallaght. In more recent times I have had the opportunity to write about lectio divina and the Eucharist for *Spirituality*. I have been particularly interested in the contribution of lectio divina to the liturgical homily, so I welcomed the opportunity to write about this in *The Pastoral Review*.

I am grateful to the editors of those publications for allowing me to weave material from these sources into what is – I hope – a clear explanation of lectio divina. Never having ventured to publish a book, I am greatly indebted to Dominican Publications, for their wholehearted encouragement.

My deepest debt in this writing is to Fr Michel De Verteuil. There are many different methods of doing lectio divina today. I believe that he has made a unique contribution. His work is solidly rooted in our Christian tradition.

1 Where Have You Come from?

The angel of the Lord found her by a spring of water in the wilderness, the spring on the way to Shur. And he said, 'Hagar, slave-girl of Sarai, where have you come from? (Genesis 16:7-8)

1851

Joseph Prost was an Austrian Redemptorist who pioneered the Redemptorist parish missions in Ireland. He and four of his confreres preached the first such mission in the Cathedral parish in Limerick in October 1851. In the opening sermon Fr Prost said that a mission is 'a sermon of the Word of God through the human words of human beings. The Catholic Church has presented this Word of God in a small book, which is called the catechism.' He said that the purpose of the sermons was 'to look at the Word of God so that your hearts will be totally saturated with it.'

William Monsell, a prominent Catholic convert and member of parliament for Co. Limerick, came to the mission, and one night his Protestant wife came too. Fr Prost preached about Jesus and his Passion. Mrs Monsell complained, 'Everything was fine but why did the preacher not encourage his listeners to read about the martyrdom of Jesus in the Holy Scriptures themselves?' Fr Prost said, 'I answered that I could have easily fulfilled her wish, but who can think of everything?'

1949

We went on the tractor to visit my grandmother. It was

1949 and I was nine years old. 'Show them the Bible', my father said in a loud voice. My grandmother was deaf. She went down in the room and came back with a large parcel wrapped in brown paper and tied with twine. Carefully she unwrapped the brown paper. Underneath was a further covering of newspaper which she unfolded patiently. Then ... there it was: an enormous book, bigger than any book I had ever seen, bigger than the missal on the altar. It had a thick leather cover and two silver clasps in the shape of crosses to keep it closed. It was a wonder to see. We looked at the pictures; and the endless pages of serious writing. My grandmother's sister brought it from America in 1903; my grandmother treasured it for 50 years. It was a not a book that was read; it was minded with faith and love and reverence.

1959

I joined the Dominicans with sixteen others in Cork in 1959. In the following months we learned about the Dominican way of living. At the end of the year Fr Aegidius Doolan gave us a retreat as we prepared to make profession. He read a passage from the Bible. Then he showed that the various things that made up our lives as Dominicans were right there in that one passage. It was in St Paul's Second Letter to the Corinthians and it described his life as a preacher. It began with the words, 'Since it is by God's mercy that we are engaged in this ministry, we do not lose heart.' (2 Corinthians 4:1)

On the day we were received into the Order, in a dramatic ceremony we all lay flat on the ground and the prior provincial asked: 'What do you seek? We answered, 'God's mercy and yours.' For St Paul and for the Dominicans, it all depended on God's mercy.

St Paul went on to say, 'By the open statement of the truth we commend ourselves to the conscience of everyone in the sight of God.' (2 Corinthians 4:2) We had been told that the Dominicans' task was to preach the truth, and St Paul said that he set forth the truth plainly. Through prayer and study we were to grow in knowledge of the truth; St Paul said 'For it is the God who said, "Let light shine out of darkness", who has shone in our hearts to give the light of the knowledge of the glory of God. in the face of Jesus Christ.' The regime was strict and demanding; we were at prayer at six in the morning. There was discipline and a lot of silence too. St Paul said that he carried around in his body the death of Jesus, so that the life of Jesus might also be revealed in his body: in a small way, we did the same. In their preaching, Dominicans stress God's goodness and grace; St Paul said that through his preaching the grace of God was reaching more and more people, so that 'grace, as it extends to more and more people, may increase thanksgiving, to the glory of God.' (2 Corinthians 4:15)

What was extraordinary for me was to find that the life I was living in Cork was described right there in the Bible. As I read that passage I recognized my life in it. It was enormously encouraging: I remembered another line in the Bible, 'Were not our hearts burning within us while he was talking to us on the road, while he was opening the scriptures to us?' (Luke 24:32) Certainly my heart burned within me. For me in this instance 'opening the scriptures' meant more than explaining: it meant showing me how this piece of scripture was actually happening in my life and community.

1979

In 1979, home on holidays from Trinidad where I was ministering, I was invited to preach at the holy well in Ballyheigue,

Co. Kerry, on Pattern Day. As I prepared for that event I came across an old Irish prayer that said: 'As I walk the road to Mass, I walk with Christ to Calvary.' I thought of those people down through the ages who walked to Mass in Ballyheigue in times of poverty and misery, in famine times, and in times of persecution.

How true it was: they walked with Christ to Calvary. Not only did they meditate and pray about the Carrying of the Cross and the Crucifixion; not only did they celebrate it in the Mass: they lived it in their lives. It was then I saw clearly for the first time, that events we read about in the life of Jesus, we live them in our lives.

I had seen this in the New Testament, but I had not paid attention to it. As St Paul thought about the huge amount of suffering in his life, he said, 'I have been crucified with Christ; and it is no longer I who live, but it is Christ who lives in me.' (Galatians 2:20)

In all the troubles that Paul endured, he believed that he was living the crucifixion of Jesus. He wrote to the Corinthian community, 'We are afflicted in every way, but not crushed; perplexed, but not driven to despair; persecuted, but not forsaken; struck down, but not destroyed; always carrying in the body the death of Jesus' (2 Corinthians 4:8-9). It had not occurred to me that what was true of St. Paul in this instance is true for the rest of us as well.

He went further: it is not only his crucifixion that we live out in our lives, we live out his resurrection and new life as well. St Paul said that the reason we carry the death of Jesus in our own bodies is 'that the life of Jesus, too, may always be seen in our bodies. For while we live, we are always being given up to death for Jesus' sake, so that the life of Jesus may be made visible in our mortal flesh' (2 Corinthians 4:10).

Here again was the text from my retreat in Cork.

At the Easter Vigil we celebrate the resurrection of Jesus from the dead, but we celebrate a dying and rising that is taking place in our own lives too. We renew our baptism promise to die to selfishness and sin – that often entails a real crucifixion – and we renew our promise to live and love as Jesus did. Where ever we see this kind of living it inspires us. It was good for the people who gathered around the well in Ballyheigue to realise that in their suffering they were living out again the suffering and death of Jesus, and in their generous lives of faith and love they were living his risen life as well.

1984

In the spring of 1984, a time when I was living in the Dominican priory in London, Fr Michel De Verteuil sent six cassette tapes from Trinidad. His topic was lectio divina. These Latin words mean divine or sacred reading and refer to the prayerful and meditative reading of the Bible. In those tapes he explained that when we read the Bible and ponder over what we read in a prayerful way, we recognise our own lives in it as well as the world in which we live.

Nobody had ever told me that. Yet that was what I had experienced in Ballyheigue, and in Cork 20 years earlier, but I never connected these two experiences with the rest of my reading of the Bible.

By 1984 I had been reading the Bible for many years. I read the three Bible passages in preparation for Mass every Sunday: I searched for something related to those passages that might be of interest and helpful to the congregation, and I preached about that. It was usually a teaching about God and about the way we ought to live. I would share ideas from the Bible and invite people to live by them. God was in the Bible, Jesus was in the New Testament, and the world of long ago was in the Bible. Today's world was not in the Bible, and my life was certainly not in it.

2 Recognising the Word of God in Our Experience

Michel De Verteuil was born in Trinidad in 1929. He joined the Holy Ghost Fathers and at the age of 20 came to Dublin. He studied history and English at University College, Dublin; later he studied philosophy at the Holy Ghost Missionary College in Kimmage, and theology at the Catholic University of Fribourg. For the next four years he worked in Nigeria and then returned to Trinidad in 1963. He taught theology at the Regional Seminary and was its rector for ten years. In 1979 he was given the task of promoting lay theological education in the Archdiocese of Port-of-Spain. He soon found out that the way he taught theology to the students in the seminary was not the way to teach it to the people in the parishes. It was then that he discovered lectio divina.

For the next 25 years he taught lectio divina in Trinidad and Tobago, throughout the English-speaking Caribbean, in Venezuela, Canada, Rome and in many parts of Ireland. His emphasis on the relationship between the text of the Bible and the life-experience of the reader today has made an invaluable contribution to re-discovery of lectio divina in our time.

Central to Michel's understanding of the Bible is the conviction that God speaks to us through our experience of life and of the world in which we live. He described it in these words:

Lectio divina is a dialogue between the written biblical word and life experience. In the dialogue our experience throws light on the bible word, bringing it to life for us so that we feel at home with it. The bible word in turn throws light on our experience which is thus transformed from merely being an event to being a word of God spoken to us.[1]

The word of God is written in the Bible and in the lives of people and in the events that happen.

This may sound new and unusual. Yet the idea is deeply rooted in the Bible itself and in the tradition of the Church through the ages. St Augustine in the fifth century said that the Bible is God's second book, God's first book is the world. The Bible was written to help us 'decipher the world, to make of reality a great revelation of God.' Fr Carlos Mesters, who has spent his life opening the scriptures to poor people in Brazil, says the same thing: God has written two books: the first book that God's word created is nature, which includes 'the actions, the events the history, indeed whatever happens in the lives of people.' He says that God has given us the Bible 'that we may understand better the meaning of our life, and sense more clearly the presence of the Word of God in our actual human conditions'.[2]

Pope Benedict said that in order to find the meaning of a particular passage in a book of the Bible, we need to know about the world in which that book was written long ago, and we also need to reflect on the world in which we ourselves are now living. There are dimensions of meaning in the word of God as we read it in the Bible that only come to light when we reflect on it in the light of the world in which we live today. He said, 'Scripture requires the context of the community in which it came to birth and in which it

1. Michel De Verteuil, 'Lectio Divina', *Spirituality*, vol. 1, no. 1, July-August, 1995, p. 7.
2. Carlos Mesters, *God at Work: the Presence of God Amid the Oppressed People*, Sao Paulo, Brazil, Edicoes Paulinas, 1983, p. 8.

is lived … To put it yet another way: there are dimensions of meaning in the word which only come to light within the living community of this history-generating word.'[3]

In his book, *Jesus of Nazareth*, Pope Benedict said that if we are wondering what a particular text in the Bible means, we should look for somebody who has lived it to the full, and then we will know what it means. He gave the example of the first of the beatitudes which Jesus preached, 'Blessed are the poor in spirit, theirs is the kingdom of heaven.' The Pope tells us to look at the life of St Francis of Assisi and we will understand what these words mean.

3. Pope to representatives of culture, Paris, 12 September 2008.

3 He Is Speaking to You

> The woman said to Jesus, 'I know that Messiah is coming' (who is called Christ); 'When he comes he will proclaim all things to us.' Jesus said to her, 'I am he, the one who is speaking to you.' (John 4:25-26)

Michel De Verteuil often began his course on lectio divina by emphasing that the prayerful and meditative reading of the Bible is done for two reasons. The first is to meet God. The second is to grow in understanding, to become wise.

The Second Vatican Council said that when we read the Scriptures, 'the heavenly Father comes lovingly to meet his children and to talk with them.' Sometimes we experience this. Some words of Scripture touch us: they comfort or encourage or challenge or jolt us. On such an occasion is easy enough to believe that God has come personally to meet us through those words.

When I am introducing a group to lectio divina I ask them to remember a time when some words from the Bible touched them deeply – it may be only a few lines, or a story, or a verse of a psalm. I give them a minute to think about it. On one such occasion a lady said that words from the Old Testament often come to her mind when life is hard:

> For everything there is a season,
> and a time for every matter under heaven:
> a time to be born, and a time to die;
> a time to plant, and a time to pluck up what is
>   planted;
> a time to kill, and a time to heal;
> a time to break down, and a time to build up;
> a time to weep, and a time to laugh;

a time to mourn, and a time to dance;
a time to keep, and a time to throw away ...

(Ecclesiastes 3:1-3)

She said that these words reassure her: she has to endure what is happening now only for a while; there will be a time for the opposite to happen. This restores her hope and encourages her to be patient.

One of the men remembered hearing the parable of the talents when he was quite young. One person was given five talents, another two and another one; he was struck by the fact that no one in the story was without a talent. This reassured him that he had talents too and could use them. Often in the course of his life, the story has come back to him. He remembers that he still has talents and can use them.

A third example comes from Michel De Verteuil himself. He met with a group of people in a small village in Trinidad on an evening in Holy Week. They read the story of Jesus on trial before Pilate, the powerful Roman governor. Pilate asked Jesus a question and Jesus did not answer him. Pilate was taken aback. He said, 'Do you refuse to speak to me? Do you not know that I have power to release you, and power to crucify you?' Jesus was not in the least bit in awe of him or afraid. He said, 'You would have no power over me unless it had been given you from above.' (John 19:10-11) The villagers pondered over the story for a while and then one of them said, 'The new policeman in this village, he is like Pilate. He is throwing his weight around and people are afraid of him. Jesus was not afraid of Pilate, we don't have to be afraid of this policeman.'

These examples show us that when we read the Bible and meditate on it prayerfully, two things are happening. Firstly, we are meeting God in a personal way: God speaks to us and we listen; we speak to God and he listens. Secondly, as we do this, we get a better understanding of God, ourselves, our lives and our world. We see this in the three examples. The woman understood that it is wise to be patient in difficult times, since these times pass. The man understood that God gave him talents and that he can always choose to use them. The villager in Trinidad understood a little better the world in which he lived; he did not have to be in fear of anyone in authority.

All three were touched by some words of the Bible. Through the words that had touched them, they met God, and they were wiser because of the words that touched them. As a result, they were freer to live their lives more fully and more fruitfully.

4 Faith Seeking Understanding

Your word is a lamp to my feet
and a light to my path. (Psalm 119:105)

It bothered Michel De Verteuil that books about lectio divina concentrate on lectio as helping us to meet God, and often ignore the second reason for doing lectio. as he was convinced that this reason is hugely important in the life of the Church. We read the Bible in a prayerful meditative way in order to grow in understanding. We are becoming wise; we recognise what is good and what is evil in ourselves and in the world, and we are moved to play our part in transforming the world into a civilization of love and justice as it is envisioned in the Bible.

'Theology' fits in here. This word is gradually moving out of seminaries and colleges and finding a place in the vocabulary of ordinary people. St Anselm defined it a thousand years ago as 'faith seeking understanding'. People of faith are doing theology when they try to deepen their understanding of God, of themselves and of the world in which they live. Theology as it is done in seminaries and universities requires a technical vocabulary; theology as it is done in lectio divina is expressed in the everyday language of the people who are doing it.

Let me give you an example. I was with a group of young people in a deprived Dublin suburb; some were struggling with addictions to alcohol or drugs, others had been in trouble with the law; from their earliest years all of them had faced serious obstacles. We were reading the story of David and Goliath. David was young and slight; Goliath was a giant of a man, a mighty warrior armed from head to toe. David faced Goliath with a sling and five small stones. He faced him also with faith and courage, and though the odds were completely against him, he overcame Goliath. Talking in a group about their own experience did not come easy to these young people, but we read the story with the conviction that they too, at some time in their lives, had overcome great obstacles. At the end of the session and after the tea, one of them got on his bike and said, 'I am going out now to take on Goliath again.' As he returned to the hard realities of his life, he remembered the Bible story and understood that what was possible for David, was possible for him. He was doing theology in his own language.

On another occasion the same group was looking at a Sunday Gospel in which Jesus said 'New wine is not put into old wineskins; otherwise, the skins burst, and the wine is spilled, and the skins are destroyed; but new wine is put into fresh wineskins, and so both are preserved.' (Matthew 9:16-18)

It did not seem that these ancient words had anything to do with these young people until one of the girls said, 'When you come off the drugs you can't go back and mix with the same old crowd and go back into their ways. You have to make a fresh start.' It came as a surprise to her that Jesus described the very thing that she was doing at that time.

Fr Carlos Mesters says that the Bible is like a mirror: we look in it and see ourselves; we see our life stories reflected in the Bible stories. He was telling the story of Abraham to a group of agricultural workers in Brazil. Eventually one of them said, 'Now I see it. We are Abraham. If Abraham got there, we will too.'

5 They Told Their Story

Then they told what had happened on the road, and how he had been made known to them in the breaking of the bread. (Luke 24:33)

Michel De Verteuil makes a distinction between two kinds of reading. This distinction has huge implications for how we read the Bible. There is text-book reading and there is story reading.

We read a text book to get information and objective facts. A geography textbook informs us that the highest mountain in Ireland is Carrantouhil and that it is 3,414 feet high. Likewise when we buy a washing machine or a microwave oven, we get an information booklet that tells us how it works and how to mind it. The human faculty which we bring to bear on a textbook is our mind, our intellect.

Reading a story is different from reading a text-book. The first part of ourselves which we bring to a story is our imagination. We see this most clearly in children who enter into a favourite story with excitement and delight and vividly imagine every detail. A story touches our feelings too: we feel happy or sad or angry or anxious. One other faculty comes into play: memory; a story reminds us of something in our own experience – something that happened to ourselves or to someone we know about.

Every story has characters, at least one; and it has movement, a plot. Without consciously deciding to do so, we identify with one or other of the characters. The movement of the story reminds us of something similar in our own experience.

If God had asked us what kind of book we needed him to give us as Bible, we could have made a good case for a textbook, with an index at the back. When we needed answers and information about God, or the next life or about living well in this life, or about suffering, we could look up the particular subject in the index, and find the information we need. But God chose to give us – broadly speaking - a book of stories:

Here are the opening lines from five of these stories in the Old Testament:

> In the beginning God created the heavens and the earth. (Genesis 1:1)

> Now the Lord said to Abram, 'Go from your country and your kindred and your father's house to the land that I will show you ... ' (Genesis 12:1)

> Then the Lord said to Moses, 'I have observed the misery of my people who are in Egypt.' (Exodus 3:7)

> Now the word of the Lord came to me [Jeremiah] saying, 'I appointed you a prophet to the nations.' (Jeremiah 1:2)

> By the rivers of Babylon there we sat down and there we wept when we remembered Zion ... (Psalm 137:1)

Here are five from the New Testament:

> In the sixth month the angel Gabriel was sent by God to a town in Galilee called Nazareth ... (Luke 1:26)

> Now after John was arrested, Jesus came to Galilee. (Mark 1:14)

Now before the festival of the Passover, Jesus knew that his hour had come to depart from this world and go to the Father ... (John 13:1)

When the day of Pentecost had come, they were all together in one place ... (Acts 2:1)

At the time when you were called, how many of you were wise in the ordinary sense of the word, how many were influential people, or came from noble families? (1 Corinthians 1:26-27)

Then I saw a new heaven and a new earth. (Revelation 21:1)

Since God gave them to us as stories, we need to read them as stories, not as textbooks. That is to say, we bring our imaginations to them, we allow them to stir our feelings and evoke our memories.

We are so accustomed to reading the Bible with our minds in order to get its message and to discover its moral teachings, that it may take us a considerable time to learn how to read it as story, allowing it to evoke our memories and lead us to wisdom.

Let me illustrate this with a short Gospel passage which describes a meeting between Jesus and the apostles after his resurrection:

Just after daybreak, Jesus stood on the beach; but the disciples did not know that it was Jesus. Jesus said to them, 'Children, you have no fish, have you?' They answered him, 'No.' He said to them, 'Cast the net to the right side of the boat, and you will find some.' So they cast it, and now they were not able to haul it in because there were so many fish. That disciple whom Jesus loved said to Peter, 'It is the Lord!' (John 21:4-6)

Here are two meditations on this story; notice how they differ from each other.

Meditation 1

Today Jesus is risen and standing on the shore in the next life; we are out on the lake, struggling in this world. He is aware of us and cares about us. The apostles were willing to accept his guidance. The Risen Lord offers us guidance in many ways; if we trust him and follow his guidance, our lives will be fruitful. This is hugely encouraging.

Meditation 2

I remember a time in my life when I was getting nowhere. This went on for a long time. Then completely unexpectedly I found out exactly what I needed to do. It was an aunt, a wise and kindly woman, who advised me. I did what she suggested and it was successful beyond my imagining. Looking back now I recognise that it was the Lord who advised me through her.

The first meditation is a thoughtful reflection on the text. This reflection engages our minds and may touch our feelings. The second meditation goes a crucial step further: it engages our memory and connects the story with our experience. In the first meditation we are inspired by the story; in the second, we realize that we have lived the story.

Here is another example. This time the story is very short: it is in two lines of a psalm.

I was pushed hard, so that I was falling,

but the Lord helped me. (Psalm 118:13)

If you stay with these two lines for a while, it is likely that they will bring up a memory, a memory of something that happened to you. You do not choose what the memory will be; it just presents itself. It may be from the distant past or from recent times. It may be a memory of a big event: a serious personal or family problem, an illness or a broken relationship. It may have been a brush with death or with serious injury. It may be a memory of something small that went wrong in recent days, and yet worked out well in the end.

Each memory is likely to contain a sequence of events: a time of stress (like being pushed hard and falling), getting the help that was needed, and recognising that directly or indirectly, it was the Lord who provided the help. Notice how the particular memory affects you as you recall it. You may feel again the sense of relief which you felt at the time. There is also the good feeling that follows on the realization that God did this for you. Pope Benedict in his Christmas night homily in 2010 said that when we glimpse the glory of God, we experience joy. You may not have thought that you counted much in God's scheme of things, yet here was God doing something for you. You feel grateful and encouraged and uplifted.

What has happened in this simple exercise is that you pondered a few lines of Scripture and this has led you to remember an experience you have had of God at work in your life. What I particularly want to draw your attention here is the process of going from the words of the Bible to your actual experience of life.

Pondering the words of Scripture usually leads us to *thoughts* about God and about life. Or our pondering leads us to thoughts about what we should do and should not do. I ponder these lines of the psalm and I am reassured by the *thought* that if I call on the Lord when I am in distress, he will free me. Or I *think*: I am often in distress in one way or another and I seldom call on the Lord; I must remember to pray when I am in trouble. These thoughts are true and may be helpful. Thoughts about the words of Scripture do not nourish and enrich us in the way we are nourished by recognizing the words actually fulfilled in our lives, happening in our experience.

I was with a group of women as they pondered the story of the Prodigal Son. It is a graphic story of the young man who left home against his father's wishes, faced isolation and hunger in a foreign land, finally came to his senses, decided to return home, and to his amazement his father welcomed him with open arms. The women discussed the story, shared ideas about the forgiveness God offers us, and our need to turn back to God.

I asked if anything in the story reminded them of anything they had experienced themselves. There was silence for a good while. Then one lady said that as a young woman she ran away to England with her boyfriend. Their money quickly ran out but they struggled on. Her parents kept sending messages asking her to come home. She remembered standing in front of a confectionary shop on a winter's night looking at the pastries in the window; she was hungry but could not afford to go in. Eventually the couple decided to return to home. As they arrived in their home town, she looked through the train window and saw her father standing in the station. 'He will kill me,' she said. The boyfriend got out first and went to him. The father said, 'At least you are man enough to face me.' He brought them back to his house.

As she told us this story it may not have been immediately clear to her what the connection was between her story and the Bible story. Though the stories were not identical in every detail, in fact she had lived the story of the prodigal son. The most touching thing in the Bible story is the extraordinary graciousness and love of the father who welcomed the prodigal home. Jesus told the story to show how gracious and loving God is; this lady had experienced that graciousness and love in her own father on that day. It may not have occurred to her until now that this dramatic event had anything much to do with God. As she pondered it in the light of the Bible story, she saw the same gracious forgiveness. She now had an understanding of God's love and forgiveness which she could not have got from a sharing of ideas about God.

6 First Stage of Lectio Divina
Reading

We read a passage slowly, reverently, several times. Our attitude is one of openness and listening. We allow ourselves to enjoy the story, to grow to love the story and to love the words of the text. The first time we read the passage, we read it in order to make sense out of it. Often enough we may be puzzled or baffled by something and we may need to look up a commentary or ask someone more familiar with the Bible.

As we read the text for the second time we divide it. We feel free to stay with any portion of the text, being aware that it is possible to meditate deeply on only a small portion of Scripture at any one time. Later on our meditation may include the whole passage. If we are attracted to one phrase, like 'Do not be afraid,' we do not isolate it from the passage in which we find it. In a particular instance, for example, we notice that it was Jesus who spoke these words, and we notice the occasion and the person to whom he spoke them. By pondering the phrase in its context, we will understand better what the words meant when they were spoken in that passage, and later in our meditation, we will recognise more clearly what those words are saying to us today in a situation that may be similar in ways to the one in the Gospel story.

We give our full attention to the text; at this stage we are not concerned with its relationship to our lives. We observe the *movement* of the passage: one thing leads to another. In the story of the Calming of the Storm, the storm rages, the disciples become terrified, they find Jesus is asleep, they wake him, he calms the storm and then he rebukes them for their lack of faith. In the saying of Jesus about the grain of wheat, there is movement: the grain of falls on the ground, it dies, and then it yields a rich harvest. The movement may be in a dialogue, as in the conversation between Jesus and the Samaritan woman at the well, from his opening request for a drink of water and her feisty response, to the moment he reveals to her that he is the Messiah, 'I who are speaking to you, I am he.'

Ideally we spend some time each day reading the passage, and we read it again before we go to bed. We spend a lot of time becoming familiar with the words themselves because these are God's words inspired by the Holy Spirit.

We can do lectio divina on any part of the Bible. It is best not to concentrate on a large amount at one time in order to allow ourselves to go deeply into the text as we read it over and over. It is usually done on the current Sunday Gospel; this puts us in communion with our sisters and brothers throughout the world who are meditating on this same passage at this time. It is recommended to read the words aloud as was the custom in the ancient monasteries.

This slow attentive reading goes against the culture in which we live. In our culture we are taught that we should have something to show for our efforts. After reading a passage a few times we may be tempted to say, 'I know what is in this now and it doesn't have anything more to say to me.' Or we may feel discouraged when we read a passage over and over and find it says nothing to us. Yet this may be a good spiritual experience if it makes us aware of our poverty and our total dependence on the Holy Spirit to bring the words to life for us. St James' advice is timely when we feel we are getting nowhere, 'Be patient, think of the farmer: how patiently he waits for the precious fruit of the ground until it has had the autumn rains and the spring rains!' (James 5:7-10).

In the practice of lectio divina we give a great deal of

time to short passages of Scripture; none the less there is a value in reading a whole chapter, a whole Gospel or Letter of St. Paul or a book of the Old Testament. The Scripture scholar, Robert Alter wrote a commentary on four books of the Old Testament: Joshua, Judges, Samuel and Kings. These books take up two hundred pages in the Bible and they tell the story of God's people over hundreds of years. Alter shows how the story highlights the consistent failure of the people to be faithful to God from their entry into the Promised Land until they were overwhelmed by the Assyrians and forced into exile in Babylon. God was consistently faithful and never gave up on them. We need to see the big picture and we need to meditate deeply on each part of the story.

7 Second Stage of Lectio Divina
Meditation

The reading flows naturally into the meditation. You may do your meditation with the text in your hands. Likewise you can do it as you go about the activities of the day. It is in meditating that you discover the link between the Bible and what is happening in your life and world. What is written in the bible is written also in our lives and world. The God who was at work in the Bible is at work in our lives, in our families, communities, in the Church and in the world.

Sometimes the text reminds us of what has happened in our experience; sometimes what happens in the course of the day reminds us of the text. In the first instance, you are reading the text, or you call it to mind as you go about your day. As you ponder over it, something in the text strikes you, catches your attention, and you ask: what does this remind me of? Suppose you are meditating on the words of Jesus at the Last Supper and you are struck by his statement, 'No one has greater love than this, to lay down one's life for one's friends.'(John 15:13) You ask yourself, what does this remind me of? Where have I seen this happening? At this moment, you are not waiting for the text to give you a message for your life, or to tell you what you should do. You are waiting for the text to evoke a concrete memory. You may recall a neighbour who has been looking after a sick relative with great generosity for a long time, and you recognize that there is a person who is doing what Jesus spoke of, she is laying down her life for her friend.

When Jesus preached to his own people in the synagogue in Nazareth, he began with a passage from scripture and went from it to the experience of those present. He read from the prophet Isaiah and then said to the people present, 'Today this scripture has been fulfilled in your hearing.' (Luke 4:16-22).

At other times you are going about your business quite oblivious of the Bible when you see something happening which reminds you of the text on which you had earlier been meditating. You see a shop assistant go to a huge amount of trouble to help a customer, and to your surprise, the words come back to you, '' No one has greater love than this, to lay down one's life for one's friends.' We see an example of this also in the Bible. When Jesus joined the two disciples on the road to Emmaus on the first Easter Sunday evening, he did not start talking to them about the Scriptures. Instead he asked them what they were concerned about in the present time. 'What are you discussing with each other while you walk along?' (Luke 24:17). When he had listened to all they had to say, he used the Scriptures to enable them to understand the experience they had been living through since Good Friday.

There are two distinct ways of approaching the meditation stage.

In the most frequently used method one allows the text to bring to mind ideas about God, about Christian living, about right and wrong, prayer and suffering, the meaning of life and death, and ideas about the world around one, and day to day living. The key word is 'ideas.' When a group follows this way of meditating, the sharing is a sharing of ideas; a lot may be said about Jesus and the apostles and the others who feature in the story. When the lives of those present are mentioned, it is usually to say what they should be doing or what their lives would be like if they did what the Gospel says. But there may be no mention of the actual experience of the people who are meditating. In this way of meditating, the question one asks oneself is: What does this text say to me, to us, today?

In the understanding of meditation as proposed by Michel De Verteuil, the questions one asks are, What does this text remind me of? Where have I seen it happen? I ponder the text until something strikes me. Whatever strikes me, I take seriously and I ask: what does this remind me of? The answer to the question will be a concrete memory, not an insight.

For example, if I am meditating on Jesus calming the storm I may *think* about God's providential care or about my lack of trust in the Lord, but what I *am reminded of* may be the time I had to go for medical tests and was frightened out of my wits. That is a concrete memory. I read the text again and I recognise that the medical tests were the storm and, yes, I cried out to the Lord, 'Do you not care that we are perishing?' I am moved as I realize that Jesus was in the crisis with me all the while. I recall the moment when he finally calmed the storm and I am challenged by his words; 'Why are you afraid? Have you still no faith?' Then I can see: what happened in that Gospel, has happened to me; what Jesus did in that Gospel, he has done for me. If I am still in the middle of the storm – if the tests brought me bad news – I may find myself still saying, 'Lord, do you not care, I am perishing?' Yet I may feel strengthened by the belief that the Lord is in the storm with me and that he can calm the storm when and how he wills.

We identify with the characters and with the sequence of events in the passage. We discover that the movement of the Gospel passage is reproduced in the movement of our own lives too. God speaks his word to us, not in the abstract but within the movement of our lives. So I ask myself, what does this text remind me of? Where is happening? The answer to the second question is: it is happening in our lives and in the world. The calming of the storm may remind me not only of the storms in my own life but also of the storms blowing in many troubled parts of the world at the present time.

8 Deepening One's Meditation

As we continue our meditation it becomes deeper in two ways: it goes deeper into our own lives and it goes wider into the world. In meditating on the parable of the talents, suppose you are struck the fact that the man trusted his servants to look after his property while he was away for a long time. In the parable we read, 'A man, going on a journey, summoned his slaves and entrusted his property to them. Then he went away. After a long time the master of those slaves came and settled accounts with them.' (Matthew 25:14-15,19).

You ask yourself what this reminds you of? You wait for a concrete memory, for example: you remember a teacher who gave you responsibility as a child and how encouraging that was; you pray in thanksgiving. You continue to meditate and then a second memory comes: you remember an employer who trusted you with responsibility. You are moved to pray: 'Lord, I thank you for that person who entrusted her property to me; may she be rewarded for her readiness to trust me.' If you are a parent you may recall trusting your children and the benefit that has been to them. You may also remember your teenager saying: 'You don't trust me!' You pray for wisdom to know how much responsibility to give. You may recall an occasion when you were anxious and over-controlling, and you pray for forgiveness.

You choose to widen your meditation

You remember a development project at home or abroad where the people are given an active role in decisions and actions. You remember nature. It is entrusted to us by its

Owner; people abuse and destroy it. You pray in repentance and in petition.

You come back to Jesus in your meditation

Did Jesus live this text? You remember that he sent out the seventy-two disciples to do what he was doing. He entrusted this work to them even though their time of training had been short and they failed to grasp his teaching and live by it. He told them at the Last Supper that they would do greater things than he had done. Before the Ascension he commissioned them to continue his work: 'Go out to the whole world…'

You recognize a pattern in your meditation. In each meditation a good person has given responsibility to others and has trusted them. You suddenly see clearly the wisdom in this and you are moved by it. This is a wisdom moment: it can be expressed in a single sentence: 'All good and wise people give responsibility to others and trust them with it.' You may be seeing this for the first time, or seeing it more clearly than you did before.

The wisdom moment

Here is another example of a wisdom moment. Suppose you are meditating on Jesus as the good shepherd: Jesus said: 'I am the good shepherd. The good shepherd lays down his life for the sheep.'(John 10:11).

As you meditate on the text, a memory comes to you: you remember one or both of your parents. You recall that though they were not perfect, they sacrificed themselves for their children. Yes, they were good shepherds and they laid down their lives for their sheep. You are moved to pray in thanksgiving.

As you continue your meditation, a second memory comes: you remember a teacher you knew who was deeply committed to her students and made huge efforts to help them. You recognize that she also was a good shepherd who laid down her life for her sheep. You pray.

A third memory comes: of a community leader or politician who was admired for integrity and who worked long hours in the service of the community, and who clearly put the common good before personal advantage. Here too was a good shepherd. You are moved to pray.

You become aware of a pattern: all of these leaders sacrificed themselves for the people they were leading. Now you enter a new stage in your meditation: you enter a wisdom moment. The insight comes to you: *all good leaders lay down their lives for the people they serve.* Michel De Verteuil names seven characteristics of the wisdom moment.

1. It is a statement; not a moral demand. It does not say that all good leaders should lay down their lives for the people they serve. It simply states that they do this.

2. It is a universal statement, it is true for Hindus, Muslims and atheists as well as for Christians.

3. It is a statement you make from your heart: if asked how you know this you, you reply: 'from my experience'. You can say it with conviction, and you are deeply touched by the insight.

4. It has moral implications: these do not need to be made explicit. In our Western culture, knowledge leads to action; this is reflected in some interpretations of the lectio method in the adding of a further step called 'action.' In the Bible, to 'know' is to love; once we truly 'know', we act accordingly.

5. It is new: it strikes us for the first time. It may be radically new ('This never struck me before.') or more often, we see more clearly what we knew already

6. It is opposed to the wisdom of the world: 'How different our world would be if all leaders laid down their lives for their people.'

7. It is open to all; the lowliest people can see it.

Lectio divina is a way of wisdom, not a way of moralizing

Jesus said, 'Love your enemies, pray for those who persecute you.' (Matthew 5:44) It is difficult to avoid moralizing when meditating on a text as challenging as this. My meditation can easily be: I should forgive those who wrong me, but I find it almost impossible to do so. If I meditate according to the method I have been suggesting, I ponder the text and wait for a concrete memory. If someone has seriously wronged or deeply hurt me, I am likely to remember that person immediately. If I find it impossible to forgive that person, I pray honestly, 'Lord, you told us to love our enemies, I cannot love this person, please help me'.

Another memory may come. I think of someone I know who forgave a relative who had seriously wronged them. I am touched by this big-heartedness and I thank God for it. I may remember a public figure like Nelson Mandela in South Africa or Gordon Wilson, who forgave those who murdered his daughter in the Enniskillen bombing. I may remember Jesus who forgave his enemies as they crucified him: 'Father forgive them, for they do not know what they are doing' (Luke 23:34). I recognise a pattern: big-hearted people are able to forgive those who do them harm. As I remember again the person I cannot forgive, I ask the Lord's mercy.

Preachers are sorely tempted to moralise. Reflecting on a particular Gospel passage they say, 'This is what Jesus did.' Then they ask, 'My dear people, is this what you and I do?' [The answer is presumed to be 'No'.] 'Therefore, let us begin to do this.' The congregation comes to church with all the burdens of their lives; they go home with an additional burden!

I heard this story many years ago. A young mother took her four-year old daughter into her local church one afternoon to say a prayer. A few people were praying in different parts of the church; not a sound was to be heard. Before she noticed, her child trotted up the centre isle and into the pulpit. Standing on her tip-toes her head just high enough to be seen, she said in a loud voice, 'You must not touch the new Singer sewing machine.' Then she trotted back down the aisle.

Let me give another example of lectio divina that leads to wisdom, rather than to moralizing. Take the text: 'Jesus said to his disciples, "Blessed are the meek for they shall inherit the earth".' (Matthew 5:5) If the conclusion of your meditation is: 'I should be meeker and gentler', you are not following the method of lectio divina. In lectio you ponder 'the meek', the gentle, the non-violent, until a memory comes. Suppose you remember a teacher who was gentle, even with the most disruptive pupils, one who never humiliated a child. She never became a principal and was not known outside her own area. Yet she was loved and respected by generations of past pupils. She was meek and she inherited the earth. Then you remember Aung Suu Kyi of Burma, or Mahatma Gandhi or Martin Luther King who lived by this beatitude: they inspired and influenced millions of people; they inherited the earth. You remember Alcoholics Anonymous, made up exclusively of recovering alcoholics, who acknowledge their powerlessness over alcohol; AA has transformed the lives of a vast number of men and women: blessed are the meek, they have inherited the earth.

You notice the pattern in your meditation: it is the courageous non-violent and gentle people who transform the world, not the rich and the powerful. You sense how extraordinary this is, and how a wise a way it is to live. Such wisdom makes you aware of its moral implications and invites you to make a commitment. It moves you to embrace this gentle non-violent way of living. To truly see the wisdom is to be moved to act upon it.

9 Third Stage of Lectio Divina
Prayer

Prayer occurs spontaneously. In our meditation we are reminded of something in our experience, then we are moved to pray. The prayer is of three kinds:

– thanksgiving: when the text reminds us of goodness we have seen, we pray in praise and thanksgiving;

– repentance (or humility): when it makes us aware of the wrong we have done or the good we have failed to do, we ask for forgiveness.

– petition: when the text reminds us of our own needs or of the needs of others, we pray in petition.

If we stay long enough with our reading and meditating we may be led to a deeper moment of prayer in which we are no longer thanking or repenting or asking, but are leaving ourselves trustingly in God's hands. This is a moment of contemplative prayer. This contemplative prayer is usually presented as a fourth stage in lectio divina; Michel De Verteuil insists that in the oldest tradition there are three stages, contemplative prayer falling within the third stage.

Praying in the words of the text

This is part of our Christian tradition: to pray in the words of the Bible. The most obvious examples are the Our Father and the Psalms. Here we take the words of the Bible and without changing them we use them as our own prayers. Sometimes we take words of Scripture and weave them into our prayers: we do this in the celebration of the Eucharist in the 'Gloria', 'Holy, holy, holy', 'Lamb of God'. We combine texts of Scripture and add our own words, as in the Hail Mary.

We also take a text out of its original context, and with slight changes, we use it to express our prayer. We do this before we receive Communion. The centurion told Jesus that he was not worthy to have him under his roof, but asked him to say the word and his servant would be healed. We recognize that these words are being fulfilled at this moment: the same Jesus is coming to us, and we are not worthy, and we pray: 'Lord, I am not worthy that you should enter under my roof, only say the word and my soul shall be healed.' We follow this same practice as we pray in lectio divina.

When we find a text being fulfilled in the here-and-now, we adapt the words of that text to express our prayer. Here are some examples from the Prayer of the Church. On one Monday evening each month, the closing prayer is based on the story of Jesus and the two disciples on the road to Emmaus. In it we ask the Lord to stay with us at the close of the day, to accompany us on our way. We ask him to make our hearts burn within us and to raise our hope, so that in communion with our sisters and brothers we may recognise him in the Scriptures and in the breaking of Bread.

At Evening Prayer on a Friday we remind the Lord Jesus that on the cross he called the penitent thief into his kingdom; with the same faith and trust that the penitent thief showed, and confessing our sins as he did, we ask that at our death, he may led us into paradise.

The Intercessions at that same Evening Prayer are mindful of the words of Jesus on the cross. We ask the Father to heed the anguish of those who cry out to him with Jesus, 'My God, my God, why have you forsaken me?' We ask him to help us to recognise Jesus in the least of our sisters and brothers who cry out, 'I thirst.' We pray that the words of Jesus to the penitent thief, may be heard again by those who die tonight, 'Today you will be with me in paradise.'

At the end of Night Prayer on a Thursday we remember Jesus' invitation, 'Come to me, all you that are weary and are carrying heavy burdens, and I will give you rest. Take my yoke upon you, and learn from me; for I am gentle and humble in heart, and you will find rest for your souls. For my yoke is easy, and my burden is light' (Matthew 11:28-30); we remind the Lord that he is meek and humble of heart, and that he offers those who follow him a yoke that is good to bear, and a burden that is light. We ask him to give us the rest we need so that we may willingly take up the yoke he asks us to carry.

When Michel De Verteuil published meditations on Sunday Gospels he always included prayers based on the Gospel text. Here are some examples.

This prayer flows from a meditation on the story of the ten lepers:

> Lord, one of the great sicknesses of our time
> is to have lost the art of giving thanks.
> What a pity that so few people come back and give praise to you;
> Like Jesus, we wonder where are the others.
> When we take your blessings for granted we lose energy and enthusiasm.
> It is only when we know how to throw ourselves at the feet of those who help us
> and give thanks
> that we can really stand up with confidence and go our way.

The following prayers flow from a meditation on the Rich Man and Lazarus:

Lord, when we look around at the world today, what
   do we see?
Rich nations dressed in purple and fine linen,
feasting magnificently every day,
while at their very gates lie poor nations,
covered with sores and longing to fill themselves
with scraps from the tables of the rich,
dogs even come and lick their sores.
Lord, we pray that your Church may continue to call
   the world
to repentance as Jesus did.

This prayer flows from a meditation on the Humble
Servant who does not look for thanks when he does his duty.

Lord, forgive us that we turn our prayer life into
   bargaining with you,
expecting that because we have done your will, you
   will tell us,
'Come and have your meal immediately'.
Lead us to that prayer where we leave ourselves totally
   in your hands,
and when we have done all we have been told to do,
we say, 'We are merely servants who have done no
   more than our duty.'

Here are two prayers flowing from the words of Jesus
about foxes and the birds of the air:

Lord, how true it is that when we are searching for
   union with you,
we can never remain still,
foxes may have holes and birds of the air nests,

but there is no place where we can lay our heads.

Lord, never let us, as a Church, deceive our members
that we can lead them somewhere where they can be
    permanently safe:
– a political or economic system that we won't need to
    question;
– a philosophy which will answer all our questions;
– a way of understanding the message of Jesus which
    gives the whole truth of his message.
Teach us to say frankly, as Jesus did,
that foxes have holes where they can lie down and rest,
birds of the air have their nests which they can call
    home,
but for us it is a constant search for where you want us
    to be.[1]

When someone shared an experience which they remembered as they meditated on a Gospel text, Michel De Verteuil would often lead the person in prayer, inviting them to repeat after him the words of the text as he adapted them to express that personal experience. This was always moving for the person as they realised that what had happened in that Gospel story had happened in their lives. The same Jesus who was at work in that Gospel story was at work in the experience that had recalled and prayed about. They may have felt that their experiences were of no great account: now they found that God was at work in them.

1. Michel De Verteuil: *Lectio Divina with the Sunday Gospels, Year C*, Dublin, Columba Press, 2004.

10 Lectio Divina in the Bible Itself

Lectio Divina in the Old Testament

In this chapter I would like to look at examples of what we now call lectio divina, within the Bible itself.

In the Second Book of Samuel (12:1-7) Nathan, the prophet, speaks a word from God; he tells a story in which the listener, David is meant to recognise himself.

> The Lord sent Nathan to David. He came to him, and said to him, 'There were two men in a certain city, one rich and the other poor. The rich man had very many flocks and herds; but the poor man had nothing but one little ewe lamb, which he had bought. He brought it up, and it grew up with him and with his children; it used to eat of his meagre fare, and drink from his cup, and lie in his bosom, and it was like a daughter to him. Now there came a traveller to the rich man, and he was loath to take one of his own flock or herd to prepare for the wayfarer who had come to him, but he took the poor man's lamb, and prepared that for the guest who had come to him.' Then David's anger was greatly kindled against the man. He said to Nathan, 'As the Lord lives, the man who has done this deserves to die; he shall restore the lamb fourfold, because he did this thing, and because he had no pity.'
>
> Nathan said to David, 'You are the man!'

As he listened to the story that Nathan was telling, it never occurred to David that he was in the story. It was a good story; it caught David's attention. He entered into it wholeheartedly and it stirred strong feelings in him. This is how a story is meant to be heard and enjoyed: we identify with one character or another and we allow the story to stir up our feelings.

David identified with the poor man and was filled with rage towards the rich man who acted so cruelly and selfishly. He knew what should happen next: the rich man should pay a high price for his cruelty, in fact he deserved to die, and he must pay four times the price of the lamb to the poor man who had treasured it.

That was the end of the story as far as David was concerned, and he would have gone on to think about other things. Had Nathan not confronted him, he would have missed the key point of the story: the story was about David himself.

At this time David was at the height of his power. He was king over all Israel and lived in a palace in Jerusalem; he had several wives as was the royal custom at the time. He had won all his wars and no longer needed to lead his army in battle, he had others to do that for him. David was the rich man in the story; he had more that he needed. The poor man was a soldier named Uriah, who was still on the battle-field fighting David's war for him. Uriah had one treasure, a beautiful wife whom he dearly loved, Bathsheba. David saw her and wanted her for himself and, being the king, he had his way. When she informed David that she was pregnant with his child, David arranged to have Uriah killed on the battle front. It was then that God sent the prophet Nathan to David to tell him a story. It was only after the story had ended and Nathan had said, 'You are the man,' that David recognised himself in the story and admitted that he had done what was gravely wrong: 'I have sinned against the Lord.'

The life story of David continues in a dramatic fashion in the Second Book of Samuel. I have concentrated on this part of the story because it shows us David completing what we now call lectio divina, a meditation on the word of God that leads to new understanding and to prayer. The first stage for David was to listen to the word of God as Nathan spoke it. The second stage was to ponder it and to recognise himself in it – David could easily have missed this stage had Nathan not guided him. David then recognised himself in the story and saw described in it what he had done. His eyes were opened and he was moved to pray in repentance: ' have sinned against the Lord.'

The prophet Isaiah used a Scripture story to show that what was written in the past was fulfilled in the present, that what God had done in the past, he was doing in the present time. He wrote:

Thus says the Lord, who made a way through the sea, – a path in the great waters; who put chariots and horse in the field and a powerful army, which lay there never to rise again, snuffed out, put out like a wick:

Do not remember the former things, or consider the things of old.

I am about to do a new thing; now it springs forth, do you not perceive it?

I will make a way in the wilderness and rivers in the desert. (Isaiah 43:16-21)

God's people have been driven from their own country and are in exile in Babylon. Isaiah reminds them of what God did for their ancestors in the past. He divided the Red Sea so that they could cross through it to freedom, and he saved them from the Egyptians who were pursuing them. Then he brings them a word from God: 'No need to recall the past, no need to think about what was done before. See, I am doing a new deed, even now it comes to light; can you not see it?'

They do not need to look to the past to see God doing great things for them, he is doing the very same things right now. Isaiah is looking at the new political situation in their country. A new Persian king has taken over and he is about to allow them to return to their own country. In symbolic language God tells them 'Yes, I will make a way in the wilderness and rivers in the desert': what he did in the desert and at the Red Sea, as reported in their Bible story, he is now doing for them in Babylon.

Lectio Divina in the New Testament

The authors of the New Testament constantly refer to Old Testaments texts which they see as being fulfilled in their own time. As they search through the scriptures they find text after text being fulfilled in the life, death and resurrection of Jesus and in the life of their own Christian communities.

St Luke presents Jesus as a Bible teacher using two different approaches. In the first Jesus begins with a Bible text and shows how it relates to the experience of the people who are listening. In the second he goes from the life experience of his listeners to Bible texts that explain and make sense of their experience.

News came back to Nazareth that Jesus the carpenter who had left the town had become a preacher and healer and was doing extraordinary things throughout Galilee. Then he made a return visit to Nazareth.

> He went to the synagogue on the sabbath day, as was his custom. He stood up to read, and the scroll of the prophet Isaiah was given to him. He unrolled the

scroll and found the place where it was written:
'The Spirit of the Lord is upon me,
because he has anointed me
to bring good news to the poor.
He has sent me to proclaim release to the captives
and recovery of sight to the blind,
to let the oppressed go free,
to proclaim the year of the Lord's favour.'
And he rolled up the scroll, gave it back to the at-
tendant, and sat down. The eyes of all in the synagogue were fixed on him. Then he began to say to
them, 'Today this scripture has been fulfilled in your
hearing.' (Luke 4:14-21)

St Luke does not tell us what Jesus said after that opening sentence. He wants us to notice how remarkable that
sentence is. Jesus is telling his neighbours that the words
written hundreds of years earlier by Isaiah are actually happening in their synagogue that morning. In the prophecy
of Isaiah, God's faithful servant declared that he had been
anointed by the Spirit and sent to bring good news to the
poor, new sight to the blind and to set the downtrodden
free. Jesus asks his neighbours in Nazareth to recognise that
this is exactly what he has been doing. What was written in
the Bible was happening right there among them.

The words of Scripture were fulfilled in the life of Jesus
in a unique way, but we can make bold to say that wherever
and whenever the words of the Bible are read and heard,
those words are being fulfilled in the life and world of those
who hear them.

Now on that same day two of them were going to
a village called Emmaus, about seven miles from
Jerusalem, and talking with each other about all these

things that had happened. While they were talking and discussing, Jesus himself came near and went with them, but their eyes were kept from recognizing him. And he said to them, 'What are you discussing with each other while you walk along?' They stood still, looking sad. (Luke 24: 13-17)

In this instance Jesus does not begin with the scriptures but with the life experience of the disciples: 'What are you discussing while you walk along?' He listens without interrupting as they tell him all that has happened and how they feel about it. Only then does he mention the Scriptures: 'he interpreted to them the things about himself in all the scriptures.'

As he does this he is explaining to them all they have lived through in these past few days, and making sense of it for them. The passages in the Scriptures were about Jesus, and they were also about the experience of the two disciples who were in Jerusalem when he died and were hearing about his resurrection this very day. Jesus, the Bible teacher, begins with the experience of the two disciples and then explains the passages of Scripture that make sense of that experience. 'Then he said to them, "Oh, how foolish you are, and how slow of heart to believe all that the prophets have declared! Was it not necessary that the Messiah should suffer these things and then enter into his glory?"' Far from being a meaningless story of violence and injustice, what they had lived through was part of God's plan: the Messiah was living out his calling faithfully to the end and was entering into glory.

When we ponder over the things that happen to us and that happen in the world around us, they may remind us of a passage of Scripture that makes sense of them. Michel De

Verteuil maintains that just as the full message of the prophets included all that Jesus lived through, so the full message of the Scriptures includes all that we live through. We can claim this because, as the Letter to the Ephesians assures us, we are 'no longer strangers and aliens, but citizens with the saints and also members of the household of God, built upon the foundation of the apostles and prophets, with Christ Jesus himself as the cornerstone.' (Ephesians 2:19-20)

He opened their minds to understand the scriptures

St Luke tells us that after the two disciples recognised Jesus in Emmaus, they set out that instant and returned to Jerusalem and told their story to the other disciples. While the community was discussing this, Jesus himself stood among them. He talked with them and ate some fish to convince them that it really was Jesus himself. He reminded them that long before his passion, he had told them that 'everything written about me in the Law of Moses, in the Prophets and in the Psalms, has to be fulfilled.' Then, St Luke says, 'he opened their minds to understand the scriptures'. (Luke 24:44-45)

The disciples were familiar with the Scriptures. Now that Jesus had opened their minds, how did this change the way they understood them? Jesus enabled them to recognise him in those Scriptures: to see described in them, his life, death, resurrection and his mission to the ends of the earth, to see these foretold and described in the books of Moses, in the Prophets and in the Psalms. He had just referred to 'everything written about me in the Law of Moses, in the Prophets and in the Psalms.' The disciples on the road to Emmaus had been given this new understanding: 'Then, beginning with Moses and all the prophets, he interpreted to them the things about himself in all the scriptures.'

St Luke continues his account of the risen Jesus and his disciples in the Acts of the Apostles. There we see the apostles interpreting the Scriptures in the way that Jesus had taught them. They had lived closely with Jesus in the last three years of his life and were vividly aware of all that had happened to him. As they read the scriptures they were on the look out for anything in them that had happened in Jesus' life. In the days after the ascension while the community prayed for the coming of the Spirit, Peter addressed them.

He quotes from a psalm whose words described well what happened to Jesus on Good Friday:

Insults have broken my heart,
so that I am in despair.
I looked for pity, but there was none;
and for comforters, but I found none.
They gave me poison for food,
and for my thirst they gave me vinegar to drink.
Pour out your indignation upon them,
and let your burning anger overtake them.

(Psalm 69:20-24)

In the last line, the psalmist calls for severe punishment to be meted out on those who have behaved so cruelly. Peter does not quote any of these lines to the community; he quotes the two lines that come after them:

Let his homestead become desolate,
and let there be no one to to live in it.

(Psalm 69:25, as quoted in Acts 1:20)

Peter told the community that in these lines, 'the scripture had to be fulfilled, which the Holy Spirit through David foretold concerning Judas, who became a guide for those who arrested Jesus— for he was numbered among us and was allotted his share in this ministry.' So not only is Jesus in the ancient psalm, Judas is in it too.

Peter remembers another Psalm, similar to the previous one, in which an innocent person is paid back evil for good:

> They beset me with words of hate,
> and attack me without cause.
> In return for my love they accuse me,
> even while I make prayer for them.
> So they reward me evil for good,
> and hatred for my love. (Psalm 109:3-5)

The psalmist prays that the evil person will be found guilty and punished:

> When he is tried, let him be found guilty;
> let his prayer be counted as sin.
> May his days be few;
> may another seize his position. (Psalm 109:8)

Peter identifies Judas as the one being condemned in these lines. He quotes only the last line because that line makes him aware of something the community must do now: 'Let another take his position of overseer'. Peter goes on to say that the community must now find a replacement for Judas, 'We must choose someone'. They pray for guidance and they elect Matthias to take the place of Judas.

On Pentecost Sunday the disciples had an extraordinary experience:

> They were all together in one place. And suddenly from heaven there came a sound like the rush of a violent wind, and it filled the entire house where they were sitting. Divided tongues, as of fire, appeared

among them, and a tongue rested on each of them.
All of them were filled with the Holy Spirit and began
to speak in other languages, as the Spirit gave them
ability. the sound of a mighty wind filled the house
and tongues of fire appeared and settled on the heads
of each of them, they were filled with the Holy Spirit
and they began to speak foreign languages (Acts 2:1-4).

Later in the morning Peter addressed the crowd that
gathered. He quoted a passage from the prophet Joel which
explained what had happened in their house that morning:

In the last days it will be, God declares,
that I will pour out my Spirit upon all flesh,
and your sons and your daughters shall prophesy,
and your young men shall see visions,
and your old men shall dream dreams.
Even upon my slaves, both men and women,
in those days I will pour out my Spirit;
and they shall prophesy.
And I will show portents in the heaven above
and signs on the earth below

(Acts 2:16-19, quoting Joel 3:1-5)

He went on to speak to the people about Jesus and put it
to them in blunt language: 'You killed him but God raised
him to life.' (Acts 2:23)

In Psalm 16 he finds a prophecy of Jesus' resurrection:

I saw the Lord always before me,
for he is at my right hand so that I will not be shaken;
therefore my heart was glad, and my tongue rejoiced;
moreover, my flesh will live in hope.
For you will not abandon my soul to Hades,

or let your Holy One experience corruption.

(Acts 2:25-27, quoting Psalm 16:8-11)

The authorities in Jerusalem were not happy when the apostles began to preach that Jesus was the Messiah and was risen from the dead. They had Peter and John arrested and brought before them. They commanded them to stop this preaching. The apostles said that that they must obey God, not them. The Sanhedrin did not know what to do with them, so they gave them a further warning and let them go. The two returned to the community and they all prayed. In their prayer they quoted Psalm 2:

Why did the Gentiles rage,
and the peoples imagine vain things?
The kings of the earth took their stand,
and the rulers have gathered together
against the Lord and against his Messiah. (Acts 4:25-27)

The psalm, written hundreds of years previously, was about a new king whom God had anointed in Jerusalem. There were nations, peoples and princes who would not accept him. The princes made an alliance against him. When God saw this he laughed at their foolishness in thinking that they could get rid of a king whom God appointed.

The community then prayed, 'For in this city, in fact, both Herod and Pontius Pilate, with the Gentiles and the peoples of Israel, gathered together against your holy servant Jesus, whom you anointed, to do whatever your hand and your plan had predestined to take place ' (Acts 4:27)

The community recognised Jesus in that psalm, but they recognised Pilate and Herod in it also as the 'princes' who 'gathered together' against God's anointed. And in this new situation God laughed again, and the community included this also in their prayer: the effect of the evil alliance was only to bring about the very thing that God's strength and God's wisdom had predetermined should take place.

What is significant in terms of lectio divina is that the first followers of Jesus recognised the ancient Scriptures fulfilled in the life of Jesus and in the world in which they themselves lived: in the treachery of Judas and in the alliance between Herod and Pilate. We as followers of Jesus today meditate on the scriptures and recognise Jesus present among us and we recognise the Scriptures fulfilled in our lives and world.

11 Lectio Divina and the Homily

The preacher needs to be able to link the message of a biblical text to a human situation, to an experience which cries out for the light of God's word. This interest has nothing to do with shrewdness or calculation; it is profoundly religious and pastoral. Fundamentally it is a spiritual sensitivity for reading God's message in events, and this is much more than simply finding something interesting to say. What we are looking for is what the Lord has to say in this or that particular circumstance.

Pope Francis, *The Joy of the Gospel*, n.154

A little girl was becoming more and more restless as the preacher's homily went on and on. Finally, she leaned over to her mother and whispered, 'Mummy, if we give him the money now, will he let us go?' Whether you go to church regularly or not, there is a good chance that you have heard a lot of homilies. And if you have, you may have often suffered as you sat and listened.

This is sad and it is not how it is meant to be. Homilies are meant to nourish us and support us. Bishops from all over the world gathered in Rome in 2008 for a synod on the Word of God. Pope Benedict published a document afterwards which drew together the shared convictions of those present. The homily, the synod said, should be preached in such a way that the word of God becomes the people's 'vital nourishment and support'.

There are many reasons why homilies do not nourish or support the hearers. In this chapter I would like to speak about one, which I believe is a central one. I presuppose that the preachers are trying to live the Gospel, are preparing the homily carefully and are delivering it as well as they can. The central issue, I think, is expressed by the synod in this sentence: 'The homily is a means of bringing the scriptural message to life in a way that helps the faithful to realise that God's word is present and at work in their everyday lives.' A lot of homilies do not help people to recognise that God is present and at work in their lives.

Many may come to Mass with a vague feeling that their lives don't count for much and that they themselves are of no great importance. How surprised and encouraged they would be if they came to recognise that God is at work in their lives; that what he did in the Bible long ago, he is doing now in their personal lives, in their families and in the world around them. I repeat what Pope Benedict said, 'Anyone who catches a glimpse of God experiences joy.'

I offer a tentative outline to illustrate how a homily may help people to recognise the presence and action of God in their lives. Here is the Gospel passage I have chosen:

> As soon as they left the synagogue, they entered the house of Simon and Andrew, with James and John. Now Simon's mother-in-law was in bed with a fever, and they told him about her at once. He came and took her by the hand and lifted her up. Then the fever left her, and she began to serve them. (Mark 1:29-31)

Here are the opening sentences of the homily:

> Can you remember a time when you were down and someone helped you up? You may recall a time in your childhood when you fell and cut your knees; if your

mother saw you or heard you crying she may have come to you and picked you up. When she comforted you, washed the dust from your knees and dressed your wounds, you recovered from the shock Then you were up and going again and ready to give her a helping hand to show your appreciation.

You may think of a time when you were 'down' in another sense of the word. You may have been ill or going through a hard time in your personal life or in your work; you may have lost someone close to you. You may also remember that during that time some good person saw what you were going through, stood by you and gave you encouragement. In a sense that person took you by the hand and lifted you up. Then you were able to make your own contribution in life once again.

The opening question takes the listeners from the Gospel story to their own experience. I am convinced that our preaching is hugely impoverished because we fail to do this. We preach ideas and moral requirements which by-pass the actual experience of the congregation in front of us. The Post-Synodal document on the *The Word of God in the Life of the Church* said, 'The homily is a means of bringing the scriptural message to life in a way that helps the faithful to realise that God's word is present and at work in their everyday lives'. (*Verbum Domini* no. 59) If a homily is to help people to recognise that God is present and at work in their lives, it needs to put them in touch with their actual experience in life.

Peter's mother-in-law

Having invited the congregation to get in touch with their

own experience of being 'down,' the preacher may now invite them to look at the story of Peter's mother-in-law, suggesting that what happened to her may have happened to them also.

There is movement in the story, several things happen one after the other. The listeners may recognise one or more of these in the memories that come to them. Peter's mother-in-law was not on her own; there were people around her. They could not cure her themselves but they knew of someone who could, and they told him about her. This may remind people of the way in which they got the help they needed: they may think of someone who put them in touch with the person who was able to help them, or they may think of someone who prayed for them, who 'told Jesus about them straight away.'

Jesus did three things for Peter's mother-in-law: he went to her, he took her by the hand, and he lifted her up. The preacher invites the congregation to see if the person who helped them did one or more of these things for them. He came to her: what a blessing it is when some one gives us their time and attention when we need it, and do not keep us waiting if they can avoid it. Jesus took her by the hand: his approach was personal and caring. Then he lifted her up. She saw the humanity of Jesus helping her up and she saw the power of God taking away the fever and putting her back on her feet. As members of the congregation look back on the times they were in distress, they may remember the humanity of the good people who helped them and they may recognise that it was the power of God that put them back on their feet.

When Peter's mother-in-law was healed, she began to wait on Jesus and his companions. Members of the congregation may recall that when they got back on their feet, they too were able to make their contribution once again to their family, their church and the wider community.

The preacher may show how this text is fulfilled in family life all around us: a husband may be down because he has been made redundant; his wife encourages him and enables him to continue to believe in himself and to have hope for the future. She 'lifts him up' so that when an opportunity for work arises, he is ready to take it. Parents do this for their children and young people do it for their friends: at difficult moments they are there for them, they 'lift them up' and those who have been helped are able, in their turn, to be of service to others. In each case it is the Lord who is at work, doing now what he did then for Peter's mother-in-law. The preacher may draw attention to the presence of the Lord doing this same thing in the wider world: he is at work in organizations that enable people to get on their feet, in development projects that help people become self-sufficient and to reach out to others.

The final part of the homily may invite the congregation to give thanks to God the Father for sending Jesus to us as he sent him to Peter's mother-in-law. All who are present are invited to join with Jesus in the second part of the Mass as he makes present the offering he made of himself on the cross; they may offer to go out to others who are down and give them the self same help which they received themselves.

Ideas or experience?

I offer this outline to illustrate how a homily may enable a congregation to recognise God at work in their own lives and in the world around them. Often homilies propose ideas about the Gospel and about our faith. A homily on this text might begin, 'As we go though life there are times when we are down. When we are down we need someone to help us up. This Gospel assures us that Jesus is always there to help us up.' Our faith tells us that this statement is true. But it is a statement addressed to our minds. When preachers use the words 'if' ('If you trust in Jesus he will help us up') or 'should' ('We should trust in Jesus; he will never fail us'), they are by-passing the experience of their listeners.

It is more helpful to the listeners if the preacher invites them to test the truth of these statements against their experience, for example, 'Can you recall a time when you were in need, you trusted in the Lord and he did not fail you?' When they remember such an occasion they are remembering a time when the Lord was present and at work in their lives.

The practice of lectio divina is an invaluable way of recognising the link that exists between a Bible passage and our experience. In the first place, lectio divina makes us spend a lot of time with the actual words of the passage. We do not read the words quickly and skip over them to find a message. We ponder them, we may be challenged or comforted by them, we may quarrel with them – in the end we enjoy them and we come to love them. We pay attention to the movement within the passage. Often we hardly notice it. If you read the story of Peter's mother-in-law with a group of people and then ask what happened when Jesus went into her house, someone will almost certainly say, 'He cured her.' Not a word about the three other things he did before he cured her: *He went to her, took her by the hand, and lifted her up.*

Secondly, the meditaiton stage of lectio divina can provide the central portion of the homily. In that stage the preacher is asking, Where is this text being fulfilled in my life and in the lives of my congregation and in the wider world? The homily that enables a hard-pressed congregation to get a glimpse of God at work in their lives and in their families and communities, will have served them well. And it will have fulfilled another of its functions: it will have given them a reason to lift up their hearts and to give thanks to God in the Eucharist that follows.

12 Jesus Yesterday and Today

Jesus Christ is the same yesterday and today and for ever. (Hebrews 13:8)

Jesus Yesterday

We read and meditate on what Jesus said and did in the Gospels in order to become aware of what he is doing and saying in our lives and world today.

In order to recognize what he is doing in the world today, we need to understand what he set out to do in his own country. It is important also that we remember that though he was God, Jesus was fully human, that he lived in a particular place and time and had to size up situations and make decisions.

When Jesus left home at the age of 30 and became a travelling preacher and healer, what did he hope to achieve? Had he a definite plan in mind and had he thought out how he would carry out that plan? The central thing in the life of Jesus at the age of 30 was his relationship with God the Father, whom he called 'Abba', the name children used to address their fathers, like our 'Dad ' or 'Daddy'. He knew him as an incredibly loving God, who included everybody in his love, good and bad; he made the sun to shine and the rain to fall for the benefit of honest and dishonest people alike. This God was big-hearted, generous, gracious; when he put on a party, everybody was invited; when an irresponsible prodigal son finally came home, he put on a party for him and there was music and dancing.

Jesus saw that if this God were to rule in his country, things would be very different. People would be at peace with God; they would be at peace with their own selves and with each other, and they would be at peace with nature. Jesus found this idea of the rule of God, or the kingdom of God, in the Scriptures which he knew well.

The prophets dreamed of this time of peace and harmony. When that day came, they said, people would plant gardens and eat their fruit, they would build houses and live in them. They spoke poetically of the harmony that would include nature too: the lion and the lamb and the little child would all play together. The rule of God would touch all areas of life, and ultimately it would destroy even death itself. Jesus recognized that he was called to bring about that rule of God, first of all in his own country.

When Jesus looked at his country, there were not many signs that a loving God was being allowed to rule there. Poor people were neglected, many were judged to be sinners and were excluded, heavy burdens were imposed in the name of religion; people were 'harassed and helpless like sheep without a shepherd'. (Matthew 9:36)

Jesus made practical decisions. He did not go to the religious authorities in Jerusalem or to the influential people in Galilee; he went to those who were on the outside, to ordinary people, to the poor, to sinners and outcasts. He told them what God was like, and he showed them what God was like. He went among them as a friend and a brother. He cured the sick, he reconciled sinners. He was not with them in a patronizing way. He sat and ate with them. He recognized their goodness and praised it: he often gave the credit to the person he healed, 'your faith has saved you'. He said of the woman whom others condemned, 'she has shown great love'. These people depended on him; he also depended on them: when the night came he had nowhere to lay his head; he depended on them for a boat when the crowds pressed on him at the lake, for a donkey on Palm Sunday, for a room for the Last Supper.

Jesus chose a small group to work with him, there were twelve of them and later he sent out 72. He took great care in training this group. He wanted them to understand his message, to live it and to spread it.

For a time all went well. Huge crowds came; he cured the sick and even raised the dead. But he began to get in trouble with the religious authorities. When Jesus saw that the rules which these authorities enforced were oppressing people, he deliberately opposed them; he cured people on the Sabbath. He would not keep rules which prevented people from seeing what God was like; the Pharisees said that he should not mix with sinners, Jesus ate with them. When he saw traders turning his Father's House into a market, he drove them out.

As opposition to him continued to grow, Jesus saw that he would have to go to Jerusalem and face the religious authorities there. He had set out to bring about the rule of God by inviting and persuading the people, now he realized that it would cost him his life. He would be faithful to his calling to the end and this was how the rule of God would be brought about in Israel and in the world.

The power of Jesus on the Cross

The leaders scoffed at him, saying, 'He saved others; let him save himself if he is the Messiah of God, his chosen one!' The soldiers also mocked him, coming up and offering him sour wine, and saying, 'If you are the King of the Jews, save yourself!' There was also an inscription over him, 'This is the King of the Jews.

One of the criminals hanging there abused him. 'Are you not the Christ?' he said. 'Save yourself and us as well.' But the other spoke up and rebuked him. 'Have you no fear of God at all?' he said. 'You got the same sentence as he did, but in our case we deserved it: we are paying for what we did. But this man has done nothing wrong. Jesus,' he said 'remember me when you come into your kingdom.' 'Indeed, I promise you,' he replied 'today you will be with me in paradise.' (Luke 23:39-43)

On Calvary the Roman soldiers and the religious authorities had all the power: Jesus could not save himself. Yet Jesus had the power of love, courage, patience, endurance, trust, and hope against hope. After Pentecost this was the only power he wanted his followers to have as he sent them out to save the world.

Jesus Today

During the 33 years of his life in Palestine, Jesus was limited to one small country. Now that he is risen, he has direct access to every person and to every place. In Palestine he could be with his disciples and teach them, but he could not enter their personalities and change them from within. Now he is within his followers, as he promised at the Last Supper, 'On that day you will know that I am in my Father and you in me and I in you'. (John 14:20) St. Paul was vividly aware of this: 'It is no longer I who live but Christ who lives in me.' (Galatians 2:20)

If Jesus is present in you and in other people today, what is he saying and doing? He is saying and doing what he said and did in the Gospels 2,000 years ago. We ponder what he said and did in the Gospels in order to recognise where he is saying and doing the same things now: in our lives, in the lives of people we know about, and in the world around us.

13 The Full Extent of His Love

Lectio Divina and the Eucharist

Loving always and loving to the end

Prayerful reflection allows the Liturgy of the Word to come alive. Similar prayerful reflection is necessary if the Liturgy of the Eucharist is to come alive for us also.

When Jesus chose to leave us a tangible memorial of his life on earth, he did not leave a memorial of his birth, or of his hidden life in Nazareth or of his public life in Galilee and Judea. He left us a memorial of his passion and death. Why was it his passion and death that he particularly wanted to keep in our memory? St John may offer us an answer. He devoted seven chapters of his gospel to the events of Holy Thursday night and Good Friday. At the beginning of that account he wrote: 'Having loved his own who were in the world he loved them to the end.' The Jerusalem Bible gives this translation: 'He had always loved those who were his in the world, but now he showed how perfect his love was.' And the New International translation reads: 'Having loved his own who were in the world, he now showed them the full extent of his love.' (John 13:1)

In this short statement St John indicates the end of one period in the life of Jesus and the beginning of another. In the first period, up to Holy Thursday, he always loved those who were his own; in the second very brief period he showed the full extent of that love. In the Liturgy of the Word for most of the year, we meet Jesus in the first period. In everything Jesus did in that time, whether it was curing the sick, eating with sinners, teaching the people, challenging the scribes and Pharisees, he was loving those who are his own. In this time we meet him as the good shepherd laying down his life day by day for his sheep. But in every Mass Jesus wants us to remember him in the second period. For this purpose he instituted the Eucharist.

What Jesus wants us to remember is the full extent of his love by which he gives himself totally. So he leaves us a memorial. The memorial is not a great temple or a plaque to be put on a wall. It is his very self, body and blood, soul and divinity in the form of bread and wine which his followers are to eat and drink when they come together. In the way of lectio divina we ponder on this prayerfully and we attend to the experiential dimension that is in it. We can see the bread and the wine, we can taste and touch them. We think about them: bread and wine are there to be eaten and drunk; they are totally for others; when their task is done there is nothing of them left. Already they remind us of Jesus. They nourish us and allow us to be ourselves. When they become the body and blood of Jesus and we receive them, they gradually change us into Jesus, and thereby enable us to become our true and best selves.

The sacrament is not simply the bread and wine becoming the body and blood of Jesus; what the bread and wine become is the body and blood of Jesus *being offered now* to the Father as Jesus offered them on Calvary. The community gathered on a Sunday morning are not just looking on as Jesus makes present the offering he made of himself at the Last Supper and on the Cross. They now enter into that offering: Jesus invites them, in union with him, to offer themselves totally to the Father. The congregation which has recalled the ways in which it has loved those entrusted to its care and has been good shepherd to them, now commits itself to love to the end as Jesus did on the cross.

At a nuptial Mass St Paul's description of love in I Corinthians is often read: 'Love is patient; love is kind; love is not envious or boastful or arrogant or rude. It does not insist on its own way; it is not irritable or resentful; it does not rejoice in wrongdoing, but rejoices in the truth. It bears all things, believes all things, hopes all things, endures all things.' (I Corinthians 13:4)

This text may already be fulfilled in the idealistic couple about to be married; in their love for each other they make present the love of Jesus who always loves his own. But as the Nuptial Mass continues into the Liturgy of the Eucharist the couple is reminded of the full extent of that love. Just as Jesus moved in the course of his life from loving, to showing the full extent of his love, so the couple will be drawn to live out the full extent of that love in good times and in bad, in sickness and in health.

Loving deeply and being deeply loved

There is a further experiential aspect to the Eucharist: the experience of loving Jesus deeply and feeling deeply loved by him. It is possible to see Jesus as an utterly loving person who has done wonderful things for us and for all people, and yet be largely unaware that he actually loves each of us personally, and dearly wants to be loved by each of us. Our experience of deep and faithful love in human relationships in the course of our lives gives us a glimpse of what the love of Jesus is like.

Meditating prayerfully on the Eucharist we may recognise that love. St Albert experienced it. He wrote about the Eucharist:

It is as if Christ said: 'I have loved them so greatly, and they me, that I desire to be eaten by them: they have

desired to receive me within them, to be embodied in
me as my members. In no deeper way, or one more
consonant to nature, can they be in me and I in them.'

What Jesus began on Holy Thursday, he continues into our
own day: in every celebration of the Eucharist he shows the
full extent of his love.

14 Lectio Divina: The First Thousand Years

Lectio divina has come a long way. I was touched to read that the Presbyterian Youth Ministry in New Zealand promotes lectio divina as part of its ministry to nurture young people in the Christian faith. For many centuries lectio divina was hardly heard of outside of monasteries; now the words are becoming part of our vocabulary. Small communities of poor people in developing countries have used it for many years; Cardinal Martini introduced it to thousands of young people in his diocese of Milan. It featured prominently in the Synod of Bishops on the Word of God in 2008. Pope Benedict promoted it for the universal Church. When Cardinal Bergoglio, now Pope Francis, spoke at the Eucharistic Congress in Quebec five years ago, he presented his teaching as a lectio divina. I would like to give a short history of lectio divina to show that it has been a precious part of our Christian heritage from the beginning.

Prayerful reading and pondering the word of God is older than Christianity. Devout Jews recited these words from the Hebrew Bible every day:

Hear, O Israel: The Lord is our God, the Lord alone. You shall love the Lord your God with all your heart, and with all your soul, and with all your might. Keep these words that I am commanding you today in your heart. Recite them to your children and talk about them when you are at home and when you are away, when you lie down and when you rise

(Deuteronomy 6:4)

The first of the Psalms begins:

> Happy are those who do not follow the advice of the
>   wicked,
> or take the path that sinners tread,
> or sit in the seat of scoffers;
> but their delight is in the law of the Lord,
> and on his law they meditate day and night.

We find the spirit of both the Old and the New
Testaments in the words of Mary: at the Annunciation she
said, 'Be it done to me according to your word,' and after the
events that surrounded the birth of Jesus, she 'treasured all
these things and pondered them in her heart.'

Fathers of the Church

Two groups of people gave lectio divina a central place in
the life of the Church for the first 700 years of its existence.
The Fathers of the Church make up one group. These were
preachers, teachers, writers and usually pastors. Their teaching was reliable and their lives holy; they were recognised as
saints. Most, but not all were bishops. They studied the word
of God, they pondered it, prayed it, lived it and preached it
to their parish communities at Sunday Mass.

Pope Benedict gave the life stories and teachings of 30 of
them in his weekly public audiences in 2007 and 2008. These
included: Clement of Rome, Ignatius of Antioch, Origen
of Alexandria, Basil of Cappadocia, John Chrysostom of
Constantinople (present-day Istanbul), Ambrose of Milan,
Jerome of Rome and Bethlehem, Augustine of Hippo (in
North Africa) and Pope St Gregory the Great.

Desert Fathers and Mothers

The members of the second group are known as the Desert Fathers and Mothers. St Antony of Egypt was 20 when his parents died and left him all they owned. One day when he was at Mass with his local community, he was struck by the words of Jesus that were read in the Gospel: 'If you wish to be perfect, go and sell what you own and give the money to the poor, and you will have treasure in heaven; then come, follow me.' (Matthew 19:21) Antony allowed these words to change his life. He sold all he had inherited, gave the money to the needy, withdrew from the locality and gradually made his way into the desert. There he spent his life in communion with God in prayer, until he died at the age of 105.

Thousands of men and women followed the example of Antony in subsequent decades and came to the desert in Egypt. In the beginning, each person lived in solitude; later they lived in communities. Their goal was to be in constant communion with God in prayer. Copies of the Bible were scarce, so new members were expected to learn the New Testament and the 150 Psalms by heart. Whether they were working for their keep, preparing their sparse meals, or praying alone in their cells, they could recall God's word and ponder it. Antony's original experience in his parish church shaped their understanding of lectio divina: they pondered the word to allow it to transform their lives in whatever way that word required.

Monasteries

Inspired by the example of these people in the Egyptian desert, monasteries were founded in Italy, the Holy Land, Cappadocia (Turkey), on the continent of Europe, in England, Scotland and Ireland. Beginning in 361, St Martin of Tours founded the first monastery in France. St. Patrick studied in the monastery of Lerins in France before he returned to Ireland. From 500 AD Ireland's monasteries became famous for their saints and scholars.

The monasteries served the people around them and became centres of prayer and worship; they set up schools, helped the poor and sometimes cared for the sick. The monastic community was a little like a modern parish. The monks were at the centre, the students were in the school and the neighbouring families worshipped in the church. These communities, at their best, pondered the Scriptures which were read to them and explained to them, and they lived those Scriptures. The word put them in contact with God, and made them attentive to one another, building up a spirit of community and neighbourliness.

The monks nurtured all that was good in the new cultures in which they found themselves. In a lecture in Paris in 2008 Pope Benedict said that the monasteries in the first thousand years of Christianity made Europe what it is. He said that at the heart of the monastic life was the desire to seek God. In order to find him, God gave us his word in the books of sacred Scripture. Their search for God in the Scriptures put the monks in touch with reading and writing, and this led them to a love of learning in all its forms. Naturally then the monasteries had libraries, scriptoria where books were painstakingly copied, and schools where the young were taught. All forms of learning were valued and seen as a help in the search for God.

An Italian, named Cassidorus, in the sixth century was concerned that the vast treasures of learning and culture that had flourished in the pagan Greek and Roman Empire –in literature, poetry, art, architecture, philosophy and law – would be lost, as they held no interest for the newly arrived conquerors. He founded a monastery which combined a life of prayer with the work of preserving and copying the great pagan works. Many monasteries – including those in Ireland – took up this work; the monks copied and preserved the writings of the Fathers of the Church and of the pagan authors, preserving both for benefit of future generations.

They made music

Pope Benedict pointed out that the monks not only pondered the Scriptures: they sang them. The chanting of the psalms was part of their worship of God. Conscious that they were in the presence of God and of all the angels and saints in heaven, their singing and chanting must be of the highest quality. Pope Benedict said that it was the monks' commitment to create music that is worthy of God that gave rise to the great tradition of Western music.

They worked

The monks worked with their hands. The Bible encouraged them to do this. It said that God made the world and rested after his work. In the old Greek world, the highest divinity would not dirty his hands by creating the world, that was work for a lesser god. Manual labour was for slaves But Jesus worked as a carpenter. He said, 'My Father is still working, and I also am working.' (John 5:17) Pope Benedict said, 'Monasticism involves not only a culture of the word, but also a culture of work, without which the emergence of Europe, its ethos and its influence on the world would be unthinkable.'

This was a Church, built on lectio divina, committed to God and to cherishing all that is good and human. We must not romanticise the laypeople, monks and priests of that time: their lives were a mixture of good and evil, of sin and grace. Yet the word of God transformed the lives of the monastic communities across the lands of Europe, and created a new Christian culture. The word was like the yeast Jesus spoke about that a woman took and mixed in with three measures of flour till it was leavened all through.

15 Lectio Divina with an Irish Accent

It is always moving to see a text from the Bible fulfilled in our own country, in our own culture and in our history. We are encouraged to find words or events in the Bible lived out in our native place. I would like to offer you a few examples of lectio divina with an Irish face and an Irish accent.

Seeing it from a distance

In the last year of his life, Daniel O'Connell was a disappointed man. A famine was raging, his health was declining, and his followers were leaving. Two of his greatest undertakings had failed: to bring about reconciliation between Irish Protestants and Catholics, and to bring an end to the physical force tradition in Irish politics. He died in Genoa in May 1847 on his way to Rome. Twenty two years later his remains were finally laid to rest in Glasnevin Cemetery. Fifty thousand people came to honour him.

Fr Tom Burke, O.P., Ireland's best known preacher of the time, gave the oration. He compared O'Connell to Moses in his final hours: Moses led his people out of slavery in Egypt, through the wilderness and to the land that God promised them. But he never reached the promised land himself; he only saw it in the distance in his final hours:

Then Moses went up Mount Nebo, and the Lord showed him the whole land. Then the Lord said to him, 'This is the land I swore to give to Abraham, Isaac and Jacob, saying: I will give it to your descendants. I have let you see it with your own eyes, but you shall not cross into it.' There in the land of Moab, Moses died. (Deuteronomy 34:1,4-5)

Fr Burke said of O'Connell:

> Let us hope that his dying eyes were cheered and the burden of his last hours lightened by the sight of the perfect grandeur of his work; that like the Prophet-Law-giver he beheld all the land – that he saw it with his eyes, though he did not pass over to it; and that it was given to him to salute from afar off the brightness of the day which he was never to enjoy. The dream of his life is being realized today. He had ever sighed to be able to extend to his Protestant fellow-countrymen the hand of perfect friendship, which only exists where there is perfect equality, and to enter with them into the compact of true peace which is founded on justice.

The dream of his life was more fully realized in recent times. Speaking of him in 1995, President Mary McAlesse said, 'Today, for all the statues in his memory and all the streets named in his honour, O'Connell's greatest monument is the foundation he laid a long, long time ago for the peace process of today and in essence the Good Friday Agreement.'

One hour of rest

Charlotte Grace O'Brien was five years old when her father was deported to Tasmania for his part in the Rebellion of 1848. He was William Smith-O'Brien. The family home was Cahermoyle House near Ardagh, Co Limerick. William was freed and returned home after eight years. By the time Charlotte was 19, both her parents had died; she lived with her widowed brother and helped raise his children until she was 35. By this time she was completely deaf having had a hearing impairment from childhood.

She was keenly aware of the poverty all around her in those years after the Famine and became particularly concerned about the plight of thousands of poverty-stricken girls who were emigrating. On a visit to Queenstown (Cobh) she was appalled at the mistreatment and exploitation of women who arrived there hungry, exhausted and grief-stricken. Charlotte was roused to action. She rented a large building in the town and turned it into a lodging house with 105 beds. She began to visit the ships with a medical officer day after day.

In order to get first-hand experience she travelled to New York on one of the ships and was moved to lobby for the reform of health and safety conditions during these voyages. In New York she visited the tenements where emigrants lived, often in dreadful conditions. She approached Archbishop Ireland who mobilised the resources of the Church to set up a mission for the protection of Irish emigrant girls.

Charlotte was also a writer and a poet. Remembering the first group of emigrants she welcomed into her boarding house in Queenstown she wrote a poem called 'The Assisted Emigrants'. These are the concluding verses:

Ah, Christ ! behold Thy lambs ! behold Thy sheep !
Within my hands one moment they may rest.
Feed, and be satisfied, laugh light and jest.
Then forth upon their way to toil and weep –

To sin perchance. These maidens, all untried.
In womanhood so childlike – strong, yet so weak.
So guardless and so guileless – wolves that reek

With scent of blood against their coming bide.

Forth fare ye, wanderers, o'er the misty deep –
Farewell, farewell! Dumb, exiled, and oppressed,
Will ye look back to this one hour of rest?
Ah, Christ! behold Thy lambs! behold Thy sheep!

A man like Synge

In 1907 there were riots in the Abbey Theatre in Dublin when John Millington Synge's play, *The Playboy of the Western World* was staged. It was a time of national revival, of the re-discovery of Irish identity, language and culture. The *Freeman's Journal* said the play was 'an unmitigated protracted libel upon Irish peasant men, worse still, upon Irish girlhood.'

Patrick Pearse condemned Synge and *The Playboy*. He described Synge as 'a sort of Evil Spirit - by their fruits you shall know them.' When Synge died two years later at the age of 37, and the play was recognized as a masterpiece, Pearse deeply regretted what he had said. He wrote:

> When a man like Synge, a man in whose sad heart there glowed a true love of Ireland, one of two or three men who in our time made Ireland considerable in the eyes of the world, uses strange symbols which we do not understand, we cry out that he has blasphemed and we proceed to crucify him.

You don't say a word

There are sad and confusing situations that cry for a word from God to make sense of them. In 1964 Brian Friel wrote the play *Philadelphia Here I Come*. The play opens on the night before 25-year old Gar is to leave for Philadelphia.

He is emigrating because he is frustrated with the work in his father's store, and because the girl he loved has left him to marry Senator Doogan's son. His friends come to say goodbye; they don't know what to say and act as if nothing unusual is happening. Both he and his father are grieved and frightened at the prospect of his departure but cannot talk to each other. The parish priest, Canon O'Byrne, arrives, as he does every night to play draughts with Gar's father. He carries on his usual trivial conversation. Gar is furious and says to himself what he would like to say out loud,

> You, Canon could translate all this loneliness, this groping, this dreadful bloody buffoonery into Christian terms that will make life bearable for us all. And yet you don't say a word. Why, Canon? Why, arid Canon? Isn't this your job? – to translate.

Hearing for the first time

In her inaugural speech as President of Ireland in November 1997, Mary McAlesse announced that the theme of her presidency would be Building Bridges. She said that in Ireland today there is 'a flowering diversity all around us.' This requires many bridges over which people with hugely different outlooks can cross and meet each other. She was particularly conscious of the people of Northern Ireland. She said,

> I think of the late Gordon Wilson who faced his unbearable sorrow ten years ago at the horror that was Enniskillen. His words of love and forgiveness shocked us as if we were hearing them for the very first time, as if they had not been uttered first two thousand years ago. His work, and the work of so many peacemakers

who have risen above the awesome pain of loss to find a bridge to the other side, is work I want to help in every way I can.

Those who had known him all along

Some years before his death the poet, Seamus Heaney had a stroke. While he was recuperating in hospital he remembered the Gospel story about the paralysed man who was let down through the roof in the crowded house where Jesus was. What caught the poet's attention was not the man who was cured and got up and went home, but the people who brought him on the stretcher. 'Jesus was preaching the word to them when some people came bringing him a paralytic carried by four men.' (Mark 2:2-3)

They reminded Seamus Heaney of the friends who were with him in the bed-and-breakfast when he became ill; they took him down the stairs and brought him to the ambulance that took him to hospital. He thought again of those who brought the paralysed man to Jesus. Their task that day was not an easy one: 'as the crowd made it impossible to get the man to him, they stripped the roof over the place where Jesus was; and when they had made an opening, they lowered the stretcher on which the paralytic lay.' (Mark 2:4) These are the last four lines of the poem:

> Be mindful of them as they stand and wait
> For the burn of the paid out ropes to cool,
> Their slight lightheadedness and incredulity
> To pass, those who had known him all along.

The poem is called *Miracle*. The miracle that caught Seamus Heaney's attention was not the instant cure of the paralysed man, but the miracle of the kindness of the people who were there for him all the time and on that day brought him for healing. The poem does not say that they were his relatives or his friends or his neighbours; twice it describes them simply as the ones 'who had known him all along'.

The poem and the Gospel story could set you thinking – thinking of the people you have known you all along. Not the ones who came into your life for a while and went out again. Not just the ones who are dear to you, but the many others who have been there through the years. You may think of the people in your own home: the relationships may not be easy always or very close, yet they are there and willing to help if you need them. I think of husbands and wives who are married for long years; there may not be frequent expressions of affection and there may be disagreements, but they are there for each other, and when one dies the other is keenly aware of how much the reliable presence of their spouse had meant to them.

We see the grace of God in those who have known us all along.

Further Reading

Many books have been published on lectio divina in the past 20 years. In this short list, I include publications by Michel De Verteuil, and by two others whose approach is similar to his: Cardinal Martini and Carlos Mesters.

Cardinal Carlo Maria Martini was a Jesuit who taught Scripture in Rome for 20 years at the Pontifical Biblical Institute and the Gregorian University. He was Archbishop of Milan from 1979 to 2002. After retirement he moved to Jerusalem to continue his work as a biblical scholar until 2008 when he returned to Milan. He died on 31 August 2012.

Cardinal Martini gave lectio divina a central place in his ministry to the four million people in his archdiocese. At the request of some young people he began to lead lectio divina sessions in the cathedral in Milan; the numbers attending increased rapidly and his monthly session attracted two thousand young people. He trained seventy of his priests to lead similar sessions in other parts of the diocese. Several of his books have been translated into English. Among them are the following.

Loved for Who I Am, Chawton, U.K, Redemptorist Publications, 2001

At Your Word, London, St Paul's, 2001

A Prophetic Voice in the City: Meditations on the Prophet Jeremiah, Collegeville, MN, The Liturgical Press, 1997

The Joy of the Gospel: Meditations for Young People, Collegeville, MN, The Liturgical Press, 1994

Stephen: Servant and Witness, Quezon City, Claretian Publications, 1993

David, Sinner and Believer, Slough, St Paul Publication, 1990

Women in the Gospels, Wheaton, IL. Crossway, 1990

Carlos Mesters was born in the Netherlands in 1931. In 1949 he and seven companions went to Brazil in order to become missionaries. He joined the Carmelites and studied in Sao Paulo, at the Pontifical Biblical Institute in Rome and at the Ecole Biblique in Jerusalem. On his return to Brazil he taught Scripture in a seminary. Since 1973 he has worked with the Basic Ecclesial Communities, helping the people, most of whom are very poor, to read and understand the Word of God. I include three of his many books.

Defenseless Flower: A New Reading of the Bible, Maryknoll, NY, Orbis Books, 1989.

God, Where Are You? Rediscovering the Bible, Maryknoll, NY, Orbis Books, 1995

God at Work: The Presence of God amid the Oppressed People, Bombay, St Paul Press, 1994

I now offer a selection of writings by Michel De Verteuil:

A Light for My Path, Dublin, Veritas Publications, 1997

Lectio Divina with the Sunday Gospels, Year of Matthew , Year A; Year of Mark, Year B; Year of Luke, Year C, Dublin, The Columba Press, 2004, 2005 and 2004, respectively

Eucharist as Word: Lectio Divina and the Eucharist, Dublin, Veritas Publications, 2001

Let All the People Praise Him: The Psalms and Lectio Divina, Dublin, The Columba Press, 1998

Meditating on the Mysteries: The Rosary as Biblical Prayer, Dublin, The Columba Press , 1999

'Lectio Divina', *Spirituality*, vol. 1, no. 1, July-August, 1995, pp.7-11

'Lectio Divina', *Spirituality*, no. 2. September-October 1995, pp. 98-102

'Lectio Divina as Theological Reflection', *Spirituality*, vol. 2, no. 4, January-February, 1996, pp. 7-12

'Lectio Divina and Contemplative Prayer', *Spirituality*, vol. 2, no. 5, March-April 1996, pp. 108-112

'Spirituality and the Historical Jesus', *Spirituality*, vol. 3, no.10, January-February 1997, pp. 17-20.

'Lectio Divina and the Historicity of the Gospel Texts', *Spirituality*, vol. 4, no. 19, July-August, 1998, pp. 210-213.

'The Search for Wisdom', *Spirituality*', vol. 8, no.44, November-December 2002, pp. 333-337.

'Lectio Divina and Personal Experience', *Spirituality*, vol. 9, no. 48, May-June 2003, pp. 140-143